REBELLIONS

DON QUINLAN

CANADA

A PEOPLE'S HISTORY

Fitzhenry & Whiteside

National Library of Canada Cataloguing in Publication

Quinlan, Don, 1947–
    Rebellions / Don Quinlan.

(Canada: a people's history)
Includes bibliographical references and index.
ISBN 1-55041-447-X

1. Canada—History—Rebellion, 1837–1838—Juvenile literature.
2. Canada—History—1791–1841—Juvenile literature.
I. Title. II. Series: Canada : a people's history (Markham, Ont.)
III. Series: Canada: a people's history (Markham, Ont.)

FC450.Q55 2005   j971.03'8   C2005-903436-4

All inquiries should be addressed to: In the United States:
Fitzhenry & Whiteside Limited   121 Harvard Avenue, Suite 2
195 Allstate Parkway   Allston, Massachusetts 02134
Markham, Ontario   L3R 4T8

www.fitzhenry.ca   godwit@fitzhenry.ca

Fitzhenry & Whiteside acknowledges with thanks the Canada Council for the Arts, the Government of Canada through its Book Publishing Industry Development Program, and the Ontario Arts Council for their support in our publishing program.

Fitzhenry & Whiteside is grateful to the Canadian Broadcasting Corporation for its assistance in the preparation of this volume in the book series based on its 17-episode, bilingual television documentary series, *Canada: A People's History*. For more information about *Canada: A People's History*, please visit **www.cbc.ca/history**.
Canada: A People's History © 2000, 2001 Canadian Broadcasting Corporation

Book Credits:
Series Consultants: Donald Bogle, Don Quinlan
Project Manager: Doug Panasis/www.Resources.too
Senior Editor: Susan Petersiel Berg
Editorial Coordinator: Amy Hingston
Photo Researcher: Lisa Brant
Copy Editor/Indexer: Penny Hozy
Layout and Design: Darrell McCalla

Canadian Broadcasting Corporation Credits:
CBC Representative: Karen Bower

Printed and bound in Canada.
1 2 3 4 5   07 06 05 04 03

Contents

Mackenzie's rebels march down Yonge Street, December 4, 1837.

THE BIG IDEA

The Canada you live in might seem fairly peaceful. Take a look into the past, though, and you'll find that clashes of all kinds happened when people tried to make changes to their lives.

Before Confederation, Canada was a string of colonies in **British North America**. The colonies were tightly controlled by Britain. Many people living in the British North American colonies wanted more control and power over their own land and lives. Unfortunately, they didn't agree on how to get what they wanted. Some colonists wanted to keep the British

TIMELINE

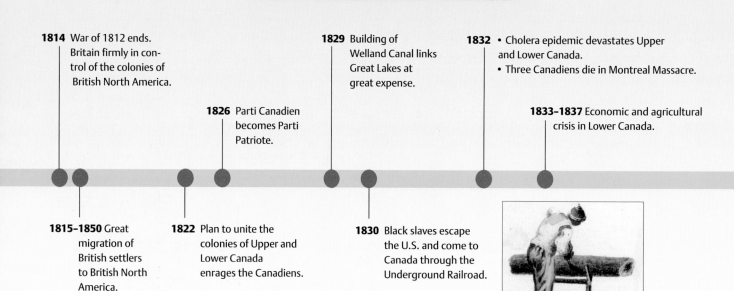

1814 War of 1812 ends. Britain firmly in control of the colonies of British North America.

1815–1850 Great migration of British settlers to British North America.

1826 Parti Canadien becomes Parti Patriote.

1822 Plan to unite the colonies of Upper and Lower Canada enrages the Canadiens.

1829 Building of Welland Canal links Great Lakes at great expense.

1830 Black slaves escape the U.S. and come to Canada through the Underground Railroad.

1832 • Cholera epidemic devastates Upper and Lower Canada.
• Three Canadiens die in Montreal Massacre.

1833–1837 Economic and agricultural crisis in Lower Canada.

Louis-Joseph Papineau speaks about change.

connection and make it stronger. Others wanted to keep the connection but have more freedom and independence so they could shape the colonies into what the majority of the population needed and wanted. A small number even wanted to follow the American example and break away, or even become part of the United States.

These groups pushed for political and social change, and they caused a lot of violence. But they also changed our system of government forever.

PICTURE THIS

So what do you do if you want to change things?

You could choose reform, which is a way to make change happen slowly. You make a series of small changes which, over time, add up to significant change. Think about your responsibilities and the things you are allowed to do now compared to when you were a baby, or to when you just started school, or even to a year or two ago. What small changes happened? What big changes do you see as a result?

You could choose rebellion, where you protest strongly against something until it gets changed. Think about times when adults had controls on you that you disagreed with or thought should change. How did you act? What

TIMELINE

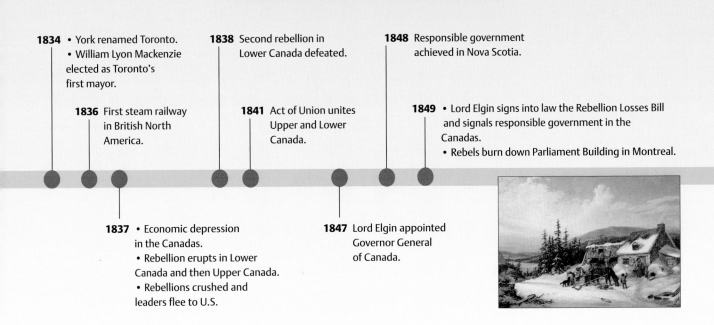

1834 • York renamed Toronto.
• William Lyon Mackenzie elected as Toronto's first mayor.

1836 First steam railway in British North America.

1837 • Economic depression in the Canadas.
• Rebellion erupts in Lower Canada and then Upper Canada.
• Rebellions crushed and leaders flee to U.S.

1838 Second rebellion in Lower Canada defeated.

1841 Act of Union unites Upper and Lower Canada.

1847 Lord Elgin appointed Governor General of Canada.

1848 Responsible government achieved in Nova Scotia.

1849 • Lord Elgin signs into law the Rebellion Losses Bill and signals responsible government in the Canadas.
• Rebels burn down Parliament Building in Montreal.

did you do to show your anger? Were there struggles or unpleasant results? Rebellion can bring change, but it can also cause problems.

One other way to make change is through revolution, creating a complete change in the way that things are done. Revolution often involves violence and it can bring new responsibilities that people aren't ready for.

Think about what you would be willing to do to get what you want. Would you be willing to take up arms or commit acts of violence?

Sometimes entire societies can act like individuals. In British North America from 1830 to 1850, many people wanted change through reform, others wanted change through rebellion, and a few wanted revolution. As you read about this time in history, think about freedom, and how much of it is good for a society or an individual. Think also about the difference between rebellion and reform, and whether one is better than the other.

THE EJECTMENT.

Irish tenant farmers **were thrown out of their homes, and came to British North America to find a better life.**

Setting the Scene

The Changing Face of British North America

After the American Revolution, the people who remained in or fled to British North America were loyal to Britain. Black, Aboriginal, or British, they were called **Loyalists**. They were the backbone of the colonies, and in 1812 they bravely defended themselves against American invasion.

The forests of British North America provided wealth for the fur trade and the lumber trade. The hard labour meant work for the new immigrants. But few people thought about the ecological impact of cutting down the forests.

UPPER CANADA

Lake Huron

Nothing represented the speed and power of change better than the building of railroads. These "iron horses" connected the widely separated settlements of North America, but they were expensive and a drain on government money.

But by the 1830s, things were changing in the colonies. The colonies were a mix of very different people, with very different needs and ideas. The French-speaking **Canadiens** of Lower Canada wanted to protect their religion, language, and culture after the shock of the British Conquest. New arrivals came from the United States. Others were desperately poor and fleeing death and poverty in the British Isles. These groups had no strong feelings of loyalty toward the British and their government.

Farms in Lower Canada tended to be older and more narrow than those in Upper Canada. Take a good look to see if you can determine the basic features of the farming lifestyle in Lower Canada.

NEW BRUNSWICK

Logging became a big industry, especially in the eastern colonies such as New Brunswick.

The ports of the colonies became very busy. Ships arrived bringing people and products from overseas and they left bearing fish, timber, and produce from the colonies. In most colonies, the merchants in major towns and ports lived a richer lifestyle than loggers, fishers, or farmers. The two groups often had very different ideas about the needs of the colony.

PRINCE EDWARD ISLAND

NOVA SCOTIA

● Halifax

In 1831, Samuel Cunard launched the steamship *Royal William*. British North America was becoming a strong industrial nation.

Quebec ●

LOWER CANADA

Montreal ●

Ottawa ●

Ottawa River

Kingston ●

Lake Ontario

The Rideau and other canals were good for protecting the colonies and for transporting goods. But ordinary farmers wanted the government to spend more money building roads.

k ●
(nto)

● Niagara

ke Erie

UNITED STATES OF AMERICA

ATLANTIC OCEAN

The Changing Economy of British North America

Along with changing populations, there was a change in British North America's economy. Forests were being cleared to be used as farmland. Roads and canals were being carved into fields and forests to help move goods among the colonies. Villages and towns were growing. Industry was booming.

Governing such a changing land was a challenge, especially when the government was as far away as Britain. The colonies began looking inward to find solutions to their conflicts.

◀ Playback ▶

1. Briefly describe the different views people held about the British connection in the 1830s in British North America.

2. Clearly explain the terms reform, rebellion, and revolution.

3. In your view, how much freedom should the colonies have had? Why?

4. Look at the images on the map on pages 4–5. List five words that you think best describe British North America at this time. What conflicts do you think might arise? Do you think you would have liked living in British North America during that time? Explain.

CHAPTER I

COLONIAL GOVERNMENT IN CRISIS

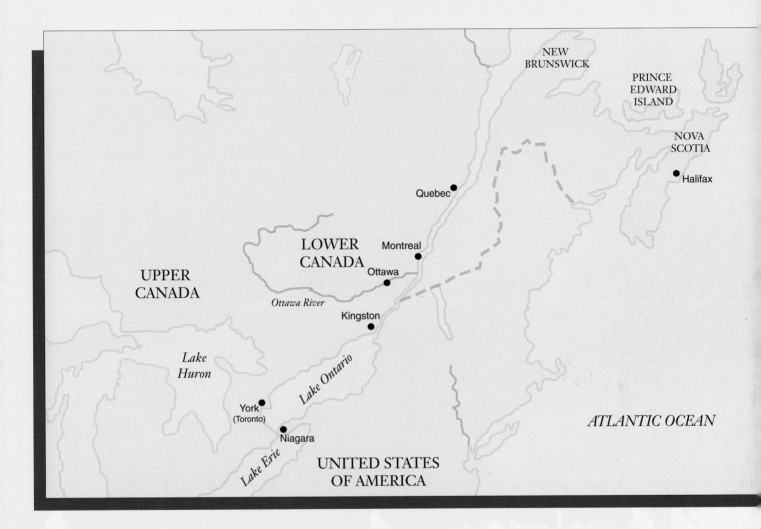

B ritish North America had a wealth of natural resources, excellent farmland, and new people arriving every day. Its people were digging canals, launching steamships, and laying railroad track to better connect the colonies. But the government of the colonies was rooted in the past and not interested in change. Elections didn't give direction to the government: they were bitter and violent and rarely solved problems. Anger, frustration, mistrust, and resentment were on the rise. Something had to give.

THE GOVERNMENT OF THE COLONIES

The colonies were growing and changing, and the British didn't want a repeat of the battles that had erupted in the former colonies to the south. The American Revolution of 1776 was bloody and violent. The War of 1812 was a reminder of the earlier, violent episode. The British wanted a system of government that would provide stability and order.

In most of the colonies, there was some form of **representative government**. That meant that some people could vote for people to represent them in the elected assemblies. Unfortunately, these assemblies had limited power to make changes or take actions that their supporters wanted. Real power was in the hands of officials who were not elected, but who were appointed by the British government or its representatives. The governor was one such official, as were his hand-picked associates and advisors. Together, they made up the Executive Council and the Legislative Council. These councils could, and often did, ignore the wishes of

Colonial Government in British North America
(Representative, Not Responsible)

British Parliament appoints

↓

The Governor who supervises and appoints

The Executive Council ←→ **The Legislative Council**

The Legislative Assembly

↑

Some male citizens elect

This is a diagram of representative government of the colonies of British North America in the 1800s. The population elects people to an Assembly to represent them to the governor. The governor and his associates are appointed by the British government, and they can overrule Assembly decisions. The governor and his councils are not responsible to the people, but are responsible to the British government.

the elected representatives in the Legislative Assembly. The governors and councils were not responsible to the people or their elected representatives. They were only responsible to the British government and each other. Members of the councils were usually appointed for life, so they had a lot of power.

Anyone who challenged this system was seen as a dangerous troublemaker. Eventually, frustrations got so bad in Upper and Lower Canada that some people took up arms to try to overthrow the system. There were violent clashes. Finally, though, there were reasoned debates and responsible government was won through words, not bullets.

WHY REBELLION?

You're about to read why so many people in the Canadas were ready to use violence to support their demands. Consider whether you think violence was justified. What role do you think leaders played in the outbreak of rebellion? Which side would you have supported? Why?

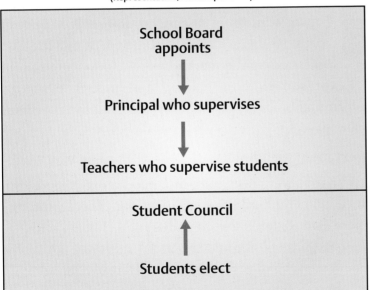

Student Government
(Representative, Not Responsible)

School Board
appoints
↓
Principal who supervises
↓
Teachers who supervise students

Student Council
↑
Students elect

This is a diagram of student government. Like the government in the colonies of British North America in the 1800s, it's a representative government. Students elect other students to represent them to the administration. Administrators are appointed by school authorities, and they can overrule student decisions. The principal is not responsible to the students, but is responsible to superiors, school authorities, and parents. Why does representative government work well for school councils? When might it not work well?

POLITICAL GROUPS IN THE COLONIES

Those who were active in the early **politics** of British North America generally fit into one of several loosely organized groups. These groups were not, however, political parties the way we think of them. As well, individuals might move from one group to another.

Tories
Tories supported the British system and were proudly loyal to the British connection. They tended to support the policies and personalities of the governors and their appointed councils. They were suspicious of major changes and preferred order, tradition, and stability.

Reformers
Reformers were loyal to the British government but thought that the colonies were ready for a greater say in managing their affairs. Reformer leaders were usually intelligent and well educated. They were not part of the elite group that ran the colonies. They believed in responsible government and worked hard to win reforms to the system. They were often successful in elections but were frustrated when the governor and councils wouldn't accept their proposals and demands.

The Radicals
Radicals were reformers who were exasperated with the slow pace of change. They were more passionate in their dislike of the government. Eventually, a lot of radicals felt that they could only bring about change through armed rebellion. Some radicals were less loyal to the British and were prepared to create a new society more like the American one to the south. In 1837, some, but not all, radicals took up arms against the governments of Upper and Lower Canada.

The Issues in Upper Canada

- **Land**

The government owned a lot of land spread out over the colony. The government sold some of the land to settlers, keeping them separated and isolated. The government was also earning a huge profit from the sale of this land. The government gave some of the land to its "friends" for free. The government also held part of its land as Clergy Reserves, meant for the Protestant Church. But only the Anglican Church, representing only 20% of the population, had access to the land.

- **Roads versus Canals**

The majority of the population of Upper Canada wanted new and better roads built so that they could travel easily between farms and small towns. But the government preferred to spend its money on canals that were built for defence and commercial reasons. Many farmers resented the fact that after the canals were built, there was little money available for roads.

- **Freedom to Criticize**

It was difficult, even dangerous, to criticize the government. People such as Robert Gourlay found that questioning the members of the government could result in **expulsion** from the colony. William Lyon Mackenzie had his printing press destroyed after attacking the government in his newspaper.

- **Government Deadlock**

Political matters were becoming more and more heated, and there wasn't much progress or co-operation. The Tories, Reformers, and Radicals fought and argued. The elected Assembly had little power and was at the mercy of the appointed governor and his hand-picked councils. Debates started to become more violent, and Assembly meetings turned into personality clashes.

- **Family Compact**

A small group of wealthy, powerful families, called the Family Compact, had most of the power and they tended to dictate government policies. They were rewarded with political power, social leadership, and economic benefits.

- **Weakening Economy**

There were many poor people and struggling settlers who felt that the Family Compact wasn't concerned about their interests. In 1837, the economy began to experience a **recession**. Tempers were getting short.

THE ISSUES IN LOWER CANADA

- **Language**

Government leaders tended to be English, but the majority of the population was French-speaking. These *Canadiens* felt the government did not have their needs in mind, and the debate in Lower Canada was especially bitter and unfriendly.

- **Agricultural Crisis**

Canadien farmers were struggling. Some fell into poverty, even losing their land. For years they had farmed smaller and smaller plots of land. Fields were not being rested, crops were getting thinner, and the land was exhausted. A wheat-fly infestation in 1831 caused great damage. From 1833–1838, there were five years of crop failure.

- **Roads versus Canals**

As in Upper Canada, great amounts of money were poured into the building of canals, while roads were neglected. More canals were good for businesses and merchants, but not for the average Canadien.

Cholera Plague, Quebec
by Joseph Légaré

- **British Immigration**

New immigrants from Britain flooded into the colony. Vast sections of territory were being settled, leaving even less land for the original Canadien inhabitants. Some felt that they were losing control of their homeland. Many of the new immigrants showed little respect for the language, religion, and customs of the Canadiens.

- **Cholera**

In 1832, a terrible **cholera** epidemic broke out in the colony. The disease began on the ships bringing poor immigrants into Lower Canada. In Montreal, hundreds died on a

Elections in the 1830s often turned violent.

daily basis. Perhaps as many as 12,000 people died altogether. Some Canadiens thought that the epidemic was caused by British carelessness. Some thought that the epidemic was a deliberate attempt to reduce their numbers and make the colony more English.

- **Political Violence**

As the problems mounted and the gulf between the people and the leaders widened, politics became more bitter and violent. In 1832, a close election between an English- and a French-speaking candidate erupted into beatings, stonings, and eventually a riot where troops shot and killed three Canadiens.

- **The Château Clique**

A small group of English merchants and Canadien seigneurs, or landowners, supported the various English governors leading the French-speaking colony. This group was called the Château **Clique**. The Clique's supporters began to clash in the streets with the supporters of Louis Papineau's Parti Patriote, a group of radical Canadiens. Some Patriote leaders began to call for a revolution and attempted to organize their own government in opposition to the official government.

◄ Playback ►

1. What is the difference between *representative* and *responsible* government? Which do you prefer? Why?

2. Briefly describe the major political groups in the colonies.

3. What were the main sources of tension in Upper Canada? In Lower Canada?

4. Which do you think were most important to the colonies at the time, roads or canals? List the benefits and drawbacks of each.

5. What made the situation in Lower Canada more dangerous than that in Upper Canada?

6. What do you think needed to be done to improve the situation in each colony? Why?

"Ins" and "Outs"

In most societies, including schools, there are groups that have more power, wealth, and influence than others. This imbalance among groups causes distrust and tension. Groups may refuse to co-operate and instead start to work against each other. As the groups grow farther apart, anger can turn into violence, as it did with the "ins" and "outs" in British North America.

The "Ins"

Upper Canada: The Family Compact

The Family Compact has been described as a greedy, undemocratic group that wanted to stop change and wanted to hold on to power for its own reasons. Whether all its members were like that is hard to say. But they supported the government and gained a lot of power in return.

Lower Canada: The Château Clique

This powerful group earned its name because they often met at the Château St. Louis in Quebec City, where the British governor lived. They tended to be mainly English or wealthier Canadien seigneurs (landowners). Like the Family Compact, they held the most powerful positions in government and society and fiercely resented change. They were completely loyal to Britain and very suspicious of the Patriotes.

Nova Scotia: The Council of Twelve

Like the Family Compact and the Château Clique, the Council of Twelve was made up of Loyalists and businessmen, often related to one another, who supported the British governor. These men were appointed for life, and could deny the interests of the majority and reject the wishes of the elected Assembly. They were particularly keen to quiet Joseph Howe, a newspaperman and a voice of the reformers of Nova Scotia.

"This family compact surround the lieutenant-governor and mould him like wax, to their will: they fill every office with their relatives, dependants and partisans; by them justices of the peace and officers of the militia are made and unmade."

William Lyon Mackenzie, rebel leader

"The family compact of Upper Canada is composed of those members of its society who, either by their abilities and character, have been honoured by the confidence of the executive government, or who by their industry and intelligence have amassed wealth."

Sir Francis Bond Head, governor of Upper Canada during the rebellion of 1837

PORTRAITS OF POWER

John Strachan

Born: Aberdeen, Scotland, 1778
Died: Toronto, Ontario, 1867

To some, John Strachan was the inspirational leader of the Family Compact. He wasn't born wealthy, but he did well in Upper Canada and lived in the finest home in York, dubbed "The Palace."

Strachan was the first Anglican bishop of Toronto. He was also central to education in the colony. He was appointed in 1823 to head the new Board of Education, was the first president of King's College (later the University of Toronto), and founded Trinity College in 1850. Strachan was also a member of both the Executive and Legislative Councils, where he guided new governors and frustrated the reformers for 20 years.

Strachan was respected for his bravery, too. When the Americans seized York in the War of 1812, Strachan stayed. He negotiated with the invaders and spared the city the full brunt of the American attack. In the cholera outbreaks of the 1830s, Strachan did much to help the suffering.

With his views on the leadership of the Anglican Church, the strength of the British connection and the belief in the leadership of the few, Strachan was a powerful symbol of the Family Compact.

John Molson

Born: Spalding, England, 1763
Died: St. Marguérite, Quebec, 1836

The Molson name is famous in Canada because of its connection to beer and hockey. But the first important member of this famous Canadian family was part of the Château Clique. Molson arrived in Canada from Scotland in 1782 and threw himself into the bustling economic life of the growing colony. In 1786 he bought a brewery and with its success he soon launched enterprises in banking, shipbuilding, lumber, hotels, and eventually, railroads. He was one of Canada's first tycoons. He became the president of the Bank of Montreal in 1826. Political power followed economic power and he was appointed to the Legislative Council in 1832.

"Steaming Sam" Sir Samuel Cunard

Born: Halifax, Nova Scotia, 1787
Died: London, England, 1865

Cunard is one of the most famous names in Canadian business history and in commercial sea navigation. Samuel Cunard was born into a Loyalist family and extended his business interests to include lumber, banking, and shipbuilding. As a leading member of the colony, he was appointed to the Council of Twelve and served from 1830–1838. He won a contract to deliver mail to and from England. He established the world's first transatlantic steamship line and won high praise for its regularity and safety. His ships helped Britain during the Crimean War. Cunard was proud of the fact that his line never lost a passenger. His company prospered for another century and launched such famous luxury liners as the *Queen Mary* and *Queen Elizabeth*.

THE "OUTS"

There were a lot more "outs" than "ins" in the colonies of British North America. They included:

- **Aboriginal peoples:** Most were living on reserves or areas far from the places where decisions were made. Even though they were the original inhabitants of the colonies and many had helped Britain during the War of 1812, Aboriginals held almost no political rights.

- **Women:** Women were a large part of the population but by tradition they did not have political rights. When some female property owners tried to vote, men restricted their rights. Women wouldn't get the vote until the 20th century.

- **Poor people:** People who had no property had no vote. Thousands of potential voters in each colony were left out of the political process.

- **People originally from the United States:** After the War of 1812, settlers from the United States were treated with suspicion and denied the right to vote.

- **Farmers:** Most farmers who owned land could vote, but they were so far from **polling stations** that they couldn't take the time to make the trip. Being far away meant farmers had trouble keeping up with current events, too. In Lower Canada, farmers were even farther "out." Farms were often poor providers and many farmers sold their land (and lost their vote) to pay their debts.

- **Reformers:** They voted and held office but they didn't have much real power because they were usually ignored by the governor and councils. Despite being "in" the political process, these men were "out" of the circles of power.

- **Fishers and loggers:** Fishers and loggers, particularly those in Nova Scotia, were far away from the centres of power of the colonies. They couldn't do much to influence the government.

Telling Their Stories

In Upper and Lower Canada, everyone had a story. Watch *Canada: A People's History*, Episode 7: "Rebellion and Reform," (04:29 to 15:02). View the stories of the Aboriginals, of Robert Davis, and of Louis Duquet and his wife. Why are their stories good examples of the problems that most people faced at this time? Dramatize or create an art work to show the frustration of one of these people, and how that frustration might grow into rebellion.

THREE ANGRY MEN

The demand for change was loudest and most aggressive in Upper Canada, Lower Canada, and Nova Scotia. Three men, all excellent speakers and writers, pushed their communities toward change and conflict.

William Lyon Mackenzie: The Firebrand

Born: Aberdeen, Scotland, 1795
Died: Toronto, Canada West, 1861

Mackenzie came to Canada in 1820. He started a series of small businesses and sold clothes, groceries, books, and medicines before deciding to start a newspaper, the *Colonial Advocate*, in 1824. He had no previous experience in the newspaper business but soon became a major voice in Upper Canada. His fiery attacks on the British governors, the Family Compact, and stories about scandals and murders soon brought him attention and readers.

To those who wanted change, Mackenzie's criticism and near-violent name-calling made him a hero. To those in power, he was a dangerous rabble-rouser.

His enemies even hired people to destroy Mackenzie's printing press, but that just made him more popular. Once elected to the Legislative Assembly, he kept attacking the Family Compact, and was expelled several times. In 1834, he was elected the first mayor of Toronto.

Louis-Joseph Papineau: The Patriot

Born: Montreal, Lower Canada, 1786
Died: Montebello, Quebec, 1871

Born to a powerful family, Louis-Joseph Papineau always showed promise as a leader. He was elected to the Legislative Assembly in 1809 and was present at the Battle of Detroit in the War of 1812. He was elected as Speaker of the Legislative Assembly in 1815 and appointed to the Executive Council in 1820.

But Papineau didn't trust the government to make changes that would benefit *les Canadiens*, the French-speaking majority in Lower Canada. In 1826 he formed a radical party called Le Parti Patriote. "Les Patriotes" swept to victory in 1834. The party presented to the government a series of demands for changing how the province was governed. The demands were rejected, pushing the colony closer to violence.

Joseph Howe: The Survivor

Born: Halifax, Nova Scotia, 1804
Died: Halifax, Nova Scotia, 1873

Like the others, Howe was a fiery orator and passionate writer. He, too, demanded reform and change. He began working in a printing office when he was just 13 years old. In 1828, he bought his own newspaper, the *Novascotian*, and like Mackenzie and Papineau launched a series of blistering attacks on the government of his colony. His tough words resulted in a **libel** trial, but he was acquitted and became even more popular. His harsh comments forced him to fight two **duels**, both of which he survived. In 1836, he was elected to the colonial legislature where he became a thorn in the side of the government. Despite his passion, Howe never accepted violence as the way to bring change. He pushed for reform and soon saw his changes accepted in Nova Scotia before change came to any other colony in British North America.

THE SILENCED CRITICS

Criticizing the members or the policies of the Château Clique or Family Compact was dangerous. Those in power were always ready to silence those who opposed them.

In Upper Canada in 1819, a Scottish immigrant, Robert Gourlay, organized a survey of public opinion about land issues in Upper Canada. He was found guilty of **sedition** (doing something that causes rebellion against the government) and banished from the colony.

Pierre Bédard was a well-educated, elected member of the Legislative Assembly of Lower Canada. He was thrown into prison for a year because of statements he made in his newspaper *Le Canadien*. Bédard actually stayed in jail longer than he had to — he was working on an algebra problem that he wanted to complete.

Robert Gourlay

Pierre Bédard

◀ Playback ▶

1. In your opinion, is there a group like one of the "ins" in Canada today? Explain.

2. Which groups were the "outs" in the colonies? To which would you have given more power? Why?

3. What is the result for each of the "outs" of being outside the political process? How have things changed for each group today?

4. Do you approve or disapprove of the actions of Mackenzie, Papineau, and Howe? Explain.

5. How should a society deal with people who are harsh critics?

6. How are leaders selected in your school? Explain whether you think the process is fair and what, if anything, you would do to change it.

From the Sources

"Canada is the land of hope; here everything is new; everything going forward; it is scarcely possible for arts, sciences, agriculture, manufactures, to retrograde; they must keep advancing …"

On change — (Catherine Parr Traill)

"These gatherings are considered indispensable, and much has been written in their praise; but to me they represent the most disgusting picture of a bush life. They are noisy, riotous, drunken meetings, often terminating in violent quarrels, sometimes even in bloodshed."

On working bees — (Susanna Moodie)

"Even a labouring man, though he has bought land of his own, is often, I may say generally, obliged to hire out work for the first year or two, to earn sufficient for the maintenance of his family; and even so many of them suffer much privation before they reap their reward."

On hard work — (Susanna Moodie)

DAILY LIFE IN UPPER CANADA: LADIES OF THE BACKWOODS

Most of what we know about life in Upper Canada is thanks to the observations and writings of two sisters who came to Canada in 1832. Both well educated, these women married English officers who came to Canada to improve their fortunes.

Catherine Parr Traill and Susanna Moodie struggled in the backwoods trying to establish farms. They recorded their triumphs and their tragedies and described a society in change. Their writings are an invaluable and vivid historical resource. They wrote adult fiction, children's fiction, books for emigrants, anti-slavery articles. No matter how tiring their work in fields and forests, they found time to write. Moodie describes what they used for light: "old rags dipped into pork lard and

ROUGHING IT IN THE BUSH;

OR,

LIFE IN CANADA.

BY SUSANNA MOODIE.

I sketch from Nature, and the picture's true;
Whate'er the subject, whether grave or gay,
Painful experience in a distant land
Made it mine own.

IN TWO VOLUMES.

VOL. II.

LONDON:
RICHARD BENTLEY, 8, NEW BURLINGTON STR
Publisher in Ordinary to Her Majesty.
1852.

Susanna Moodie

stuffed into the mouth of a bottle." The two women became literary legends and helped create a special Canadian literature closely tied to the description of the land.

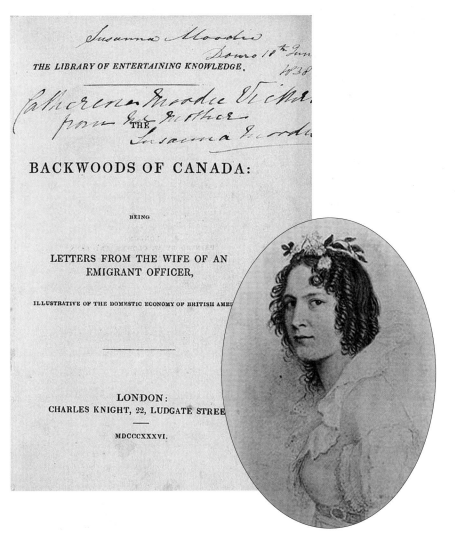

THE LIBRARY OF ENTERTAINING KNOWLEDGE.

BACKWOODS OF CANADA:

BEING

LETTERS FROM THE WIFE OF AN EMIGRANT OFFICER,

ILLUSTRATIVE OF THE DOMESTIC ECONOMY OF BRITISH AMER

LONDON:
CHARLES KNIGHT, 22, LUDGATE STREE

MDCCCXXXVI.

Catherine Parr Traill

From the Sources

"The insects are troublesome, particularly the black flies. You do not feel their bite until you see a stream of blood flowing from the wound. Later it starts to swell and itch. These 'beasties' delight in biting your throat, ears and cheeks."

On black flies — (Catherine Parr Traill)

"Nothing can be more comfortless than some of these shanties, reeking with smoke and dirt, the common receptacle for children, pigs and fowls."

On housing — (Catherine Parr Traill)

"I must say for all its roughness, I love Canada, and am as happy in my humble loghouse as if it were a courtly hall or bower."

On housing — (Catherine Parr Traill)

◀ Playback ▶

1. What are the positive and negative traits that Catherine Parr Traill and Susanna Moodie find in Canada?

2. Which traits do you think most accurately describe Canada today? Explain.

3. How does reading about daily life in Upper Canada help you understand the reasons that people were pushing for change in government?

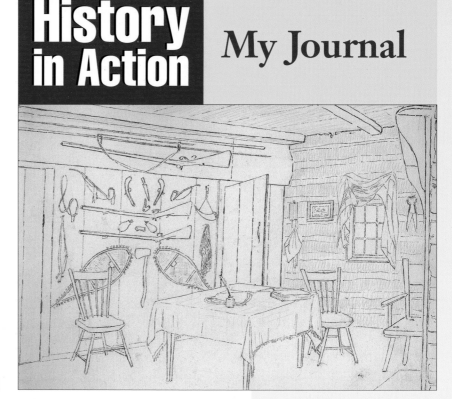

History in Action   My Journal

The Back Story

Susanna Moodie and Catherine Parr Traill made a huge contribution to Canadian literature and history as they recorded the creation of a new society. Artist Anne Langton, like other pioneer women, added to that record by creating visuals of life in pioneer homes.

The Goal

In a historical role of your choice, write a journal of observations on life in British North America based on your reading of the opening sections of this book. You may also consult other sources in your classroom, the library, and the Internet.

Anne Langton's sketch of one view inside her family's cabin near Peterborough in 1837

The Steps

1. Review the introduction and the first chapter of this book.
2. Choose the role you will take to write your journal: your age, gender, and position in life.
3. Write at least five journal entries, each at least one paragraph long, commenting on your experiences and reflections on life in the growing colonies. Use appropriate dates to identify your writings. Illustrate your journal entries if you wish.
4. Have a peer or adult comment on your first draft, then complete a final version of your journal.

Evaluating Your Work

These are the criteria you should think about as you complete your work. Your work should:

- Be based on a good understanding of the time period
- Reflect accurately daily life of the time period
- Include five entries of at least one paragraph each
- Show the results of having been reviewed by at least one person
- Be neatly presented and free of spelling and grammar errors

CHAPTER 2

REBELLION EXPLODES IN LOWER CANADA

The Insurgents at Beauharnois
by Katherine Jane Ellice

Katherine Jane Ellice was at her father-in-law's seigneury at Beauharnois when it was attacked on November 4, 1838. She was kept prisoner there with her sister Tina (Miss Eglantine Balfour) and other members of the household until November 10, when they were freed by troops. She created this painting describing what she saw. How do you think you would feel in her place?

Let's review what we know so far. The colonies of British North America are growing and changing quickly. A small group of people hold most of the power over the larger population. In all of the colonies, people are pushing for changes to the way things are run. There are lots of big issues — from land use to government spending to the system of government. There are many groups involved, all of whom have different ideas. So who and what led to rebellion in Lower Canada?

"In the long running political stand-off in Lower Canada, words failed and guns spoke in the fall of 1837."

John Thompson, *Horizon Canada,* **no.34, p.793**

ON THE ROAD TO WAR

• Political Deadlock

Although the Patriotes controlled the Assembly, they could not bend the governor and the Château Clique to their will. Their bills were rejected, so they refused to give the government the money it needed to function. This resulted in a bitter, stubborn deadlock where neither side would compromise. Finally, Britain allowed the governor to take funds without the approval of the Assembly. Eventually, in frustration, the governor dissolved the Assembly. This was the last straw for some Patriotes. They resolved to take matters into their own hands.

"Henceforth, there must be no peace in the province, Agitate! Agitate! Agitate!"

The Vindicator, **Patriote newspaper**

• A Summer of Rallies and Protests

When it was clear that the governor and Château Clique would never accept rule by the elected majority in the Legislative Assembly, Patriote leaders moved into the

In the countryside, Patriote leaders seemed to be preparing an American-style revolution.

countryside to organize their own form of representative government. All through the summer and fall of 1837, Patriotes and their supporters held rallies and protests attacking the government. At large meetings, they urged people to vote for their own officials and reject those chosen by the governor and Château Clique. They voted to **boycott** British goods and wear homemade cloth. They declared their right to abolish the government.

One leader, Wolfred Nelson, told the crowd that the time had come for more direct action.

"Well I believe that the moment has come to melt down our tin plates and tin spoons and forge them into bullets."

This made the authorities more worried — and angry.

• Gang Warfare in the Streets

For months, Patriotes and Tories harassed each other in the streets of Montreal. Two "gangs" were organized. The Doric Club was a group of young English Tories. They thought the Patriotes were disloyal troublemakers. The Fils de Liberté (Sons of Liberty) took their name from the radicals who launched the American Revolution. They felt that the British had forced them to give up their rights, language, and customs. Members of both groups were young and hot-headed, and eager to settle things with their fists. They were tired of political debates — they wanted action. The night of November 6, 1837, their taunting and insults exploded into brutal beatings on the pavement. Stones whizzed in the air and clubs were whirled about. Homes were vandalized and the leader of "Les Fils" was beaten and blinded in one eye.

Afraid of an uprising, the goverment sent out the army to arrest the Patriote leaders. Rather than be arrested and imprisoned, the Patriotes fled to the countryside where they knew they would be safe. British forces thought the Patriote flight was an attempt to build up forces before an attack.

Murder Among Gentlemen

Although illegal, duelling was still practiced in the British colonies. Many aspects of life in British North America, including politics, were pretty rough. The fighting wasn't just between gangs of young men, either. Gentlemen settled disputes of all kinds in duels. People duelled to defend themselves from accusations, or to uphold their own honour or the honour of others. There are at least 300 incidents of duels being fought on Canadian soil, with the last fatal one being recorded in Lower Canada in 1838.

Some famous Canadian politicians survived duels: James Douglas (first governor of British Columbia), Joseph Howe (premier of Nova Scotia and federal cabinet minister), and George Cartier (a Father of Confederation).

Telling Their Stories

Julie Papineau was Louis-Joseph Papineau's wife. Watch *Canada: A People's History*, Episode 7: "Rebellion and Reform, A Seething Anger" (hr. 0, 31:45 to 36:52), "The Last Stand" (hr. 2, 10:18 to 16:25), and "The Calm Between the Storms" (hr. 2, 16:25 to 26:44). Listen to the words written by Julie Papineau in her letters, and those that her husband wrote to her. What do you learn about the feelings of the Patriotes from these letters? What kind of person do you think Julie Papineau was? Write a letter, in role as Julie Papineau, describing to a friend why you support your husband and his cause, and what you hope the future will hold for you and other Canadiens.

• **Attempted Arrests**

British troops moved into the countryside to make arrests and display a show of force that would make the Patriotes surrender. People in Lower Canada were furious at the government's action. Some of them attacked the soldiers and freed the prisoners. Matters were getting completely out of hand.

British soldiers with their prisoners

◀ Playback ▶

1. **Rank the short-term causes of the rebellion in Lower Canada from most important to least important. Be prepared to explain your choices.**

2. **In your opinion, why might young people play such a big role in the street violence that broke out in Montreal?**

3. **What does the practice of duelling show about the nature of colonial society?**

4. **Do you think that the rebellion in Lower Canada could have been prevented? Explain fully.**

Three Battles – One Short War

Street fights in Montreal were only the beginning of what turned into war between the French and the English. When British forces moved into the countryside, battles began to break out. Patriotes would taste victory — and then defeat. Many people died or were hurt. Many Canadiens fled to the United States. Some were hanged for treason while others were **exiled** or sent to remote, empty lands. The memory of this struggle would increase the distrust and suspicion between French and English for generations.

St. Denis: Patriote Victory

As British soldiers headed out to arrest Patriotes near St. Denis, Patriote leader Wolfred Nelson decided to stand his ground and fight. Neither the British nor the Patriotes were particularly well equipped for war at this stage. British soldiers were rusty and most Patriotes didn't have usable weapons. Nelson's defence, though, was energetic, and the Patriotes forced the British to withdraw.

The unexpected victory encouraged the Patriotes. Many, no matter how ill prepared for battle, felt brave enough to join the rebellion. But the British were determined to crush the rebels and avenge their losses. Bloodier battles were to come.

La Légende d'un Peuple **by Louis Fréchette shows the battle at St. Denis.**

Although the Patriote forces fought bravely, they were outgunned and had little military experience. The re-energized British and Loyalist troops fought fiercely and won a brutal victory.

> "I don't know how many I killed, but I fired without remorse. It was not so much from a sentiment of insults and injustices, but the old instinct of traditional hatred of the races that awoke in us; we were fighting despotism, but it was above all the English that we loved to aim at."
>
> **Philippe-Napoléon Pacaud, Patriote fighter**

Where was Papineau?

So what happened to Louis-Joseph Papineau, the man who had stirred up his people to defend themselves in the first place? He stayed far from combat, and before the battle at St. Denis was over, he was on the run. He fled across the border to the safety of the U.S. Papineau later claimed that Nelson had told him to get away for his own safety. Nelson denied the statement. Without a leader, the rebellion was doomed.

St. Charles: Patriote Disaster

With their victory at St. Denis, some Patriotes felt that they could beat the British easily. Hundreds of new recruits rushed to the Patriote base at St. Charles. However, they had little ammunition and few weapons, and within two days, the re-organized British, along with Loyalist supporters, swarmed St. Charles. Wanting revenge, and angry after finding the mutilated body of a British officer, they charged the Patriotes with bayonets, and torched homes and other buildings. They hunted down Wolfred Nelson and captured him near the U.S. border.

St. Eustache: Death of a Hero

After they had destroyed the Patriote base at St. Charles, British and Loyalist forces headed to St. Eustache to battle with another Patriote stronghold. Thousands of British forces, equipped with cannons, blasted the rebels to pieces. A small group of rebels, led by Jean Olivier Chenier, retreated to a church to make a last stand. The British set the church on fire. The rebels ran from the burning building and died in a hail of musket balls. Chenier, an inspirational leader, was killed. Later some unruly Loyalist forces **sacked** the town.

The battle at St. Eustache

Jean Olivier Chenier   **Wolfred Nelson**

The British crushed the spirit of the revolt with a campaign of burning villages and arresting rebel sympathizers. With its rebels dead, dying, or defeated and its leaders arrested or in exile, the rebellion in Lower Canada was crushed.

Aftermath

What the reformers in Lower Canada wanted was change. But St. Eustache was in flames and British forces were torching Patriote bases in the countryside. The rebellion hadn't brought democracy any closer. Patriote sympathizers tensely awaited the full response from the British government.

Patriote Warriors: Chenier and Nelson

The conflict in Lower Canada wasn't really a fight between the English and the French. In fact the two major military figures in the rebellion were Chenier and Nelson — one **francophone** and one **anglophone**. The struggle had more to do with many groups thinking that the British had too much power and control. Most francophones weren't even interested in armed rebellion. On the other hand, some of the rebellion's strongest supporters were anglophone. The Irish and Scottish communities of the area didn't like the British, whom they felt had conquered their homelands. Neither group was happy with the undemocratic way the government was run.

◀ Playback ▶

1. **Briefly summarize the three major battles that took place in Lower Canada.**

2. **Why do you think that the Patriotes were defeated?**

3. **What evidence is there that not all French and English disliked each other?**

4. **How might French-Canadians view the events of 1837? Why?**

5. **If you were to advise the British on what to do once the fighting was over, what might you have suggested and why?**

History in Action   The Speech

The Back Story

In St. Denis, the Patriotes are gathering forces to fight the British who have arrest warrants for Patriote leaders such as Papineau and Nelson. The people of St. Denis are divided about what to do, and are going to meet at the schoolhouse to discuss joining the Patriote forces. Most people are sympathetic to the Patriotes and their leaders. At the same time, most are peaceful people and fear the anger and power of the British forces. The Canadiens could win independence, or they could lose everything.

The Goal

In role as a Canadien farmer, list the positive and negative results of joining the rebellion. Then choose a position to support and write a one-page speech that you will give at the community meeting.

The Steps

1. Organize your thoughts by completing a list of positive and negative results of joining the rebellion.
2. Decide which of the factors in your list are most important to you.
3. Write a one-page draft of a speech that you will give when the village assembles.
4. Re-read your arguments and speech and then prepare a final version of your speech.
5. Read your speech to your classmates (in role as the people of St. Denis). Be sure to show your skill as a speaker, and to share your passions and conviction as you speak.
6. Be prepared to discuss and debate your speech and the others you hear.
7. With your classmates, make a final decision about whether to join the rebellion or stay neutral. Discuss your reasons for the decision you made.

In times of crisis and conflict, the ability to make a powerful speech can be an important skill. When tempers are high, good speakers such as Papineau or Mackenzie can move people to action. Taking action can be dangerous, though. Clear thinking is usually the best way to make important decisions.

Evaluating Your Work

These are the criteria you should think about as you complete your work. Your work should:

• Include a list and an evaluation of positive and negative factors
• Include a rough draft and a final draft of your speech
• Be at least one page long
• Clearly outline your opinions and support them thoughtfully
• Be read forcefully and with skill and conviction

CHAPTER 3

REBELLION IN UPPER CANADA

The death of Colonel Moodie created a hero for loyalist Upper Canadians.

While the French and English were fighting in the streets and battling in the countryside of Lower Canada, things were not quiet in Upper Canada either. The Tories, loyal to the British, held most of the power in government. The Reformers, elected to the Assembly by the people, wanted change. But most of their wishes and decisions were ignored. The government controlled much of the land, spent its money in ways the people didn't want, and punished anyone who spoke against it. Almost nothing got done in government because the Tories and Reformers were unable to agree. People wanted change. If reform couldn't bring it, maybe rebellion could.

Much was expected of Bond Head, but he quickly fell out with Reformers. Some said he was appointed by mistake — his brother was supposed to have gotten the job.

STEPS TO REBELLION

Relations between the Tories and Reformers in Upper Canada had been tense and bitter for years. But after the election of 1836, the tensions turned to violence pretty quickly. What happened in the short term to create such a big change?

• A New Governor

First, the British government appointed a new governor, Sir Francis Bond Head. At first he seemed to want to work for slow reform. He even appointed some moderate Reformers to the Executive Council. But it didn't take long for the Reformers to realize that not much was changing — their ideas were heard but no one acted on them. Angrily, the Reformers resigned. Mackenzie referred to the governor as "Bonehead," adding to the tension between the groups.

• Election of 1836

In 1836, Bond Head called an election. He openly urged people to support the Tories and reject the disloyal Reformers. He threatened to cut off government money to public works if the government he wanted was not elected. Bond Head and his supporters trounced the Reformers in a hard-fought election. Reformers were extremely disappointed and more of them resigned from the Assembly. But the radicals, like Mackenzie, got angrier. They thought the political system was working against them, and that there was only one way to fix it.

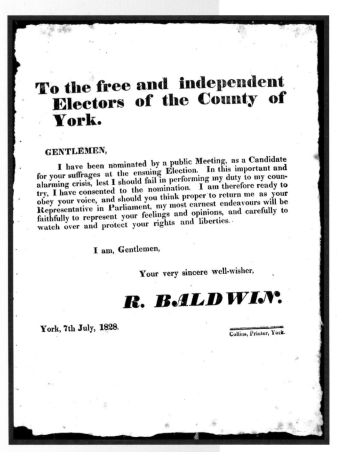

To the free and independent Electors of the County of York.

GENTLEMEN,

I have been nominated by a public Meeting, as a Candidate for your suffrages at the ensuing Election. In this important and alarming crisis, lest I should fail in performing my duty to my country, I have consented to the nomination. I am therefore ready to obey your voice, and should you think proper to return me as your Representative in Parliament, my most earnest endeavours will be faithfully to represent your feelings and opinions, and carefully to watch over and protect your rights and liberties.

I am, Gentlemen,

Your very sincere well-wisher,

R. BALDWIN.

York, 7th July, 1828.

Collins, Printer, York.

This is a campaign poster from the election in 1836. Do you think the poster is fair? To whom is the poster helpful? Hurtful? Do you think today's Canadian elections are fought fairly? Explain.

Rival candidates in an Upper Canada election, 1828

• Growth of the Radical Reformers

After the election, the Tories were in power, the Reformers were losing hope and interest, and radicals such as William Lyon Mackenzie moved to centre stage. Mackenzie's hatred of the Family Compact and of Governor Bond Head was virtually out of control. The people were desperate for change and Mackenzie's courage and anger started to look attractive. Mackenzie and his supporters worked hard among the farming communities to prepare people for action. They organized protest meetings and a few plotted to overthrow the government. Mackenzie handed out leaflets calling for the end of the government.

Oh, men of Upper Canada, would you murder a free people! Before you do so pause, and consider the world has its eyes on you — history will mark your conduct — beware lest they condemn. Oh who would not have it said of him that, as an Upper Canadian ... he died in the cause of freedom! To die fighting for freedom is truly glorious. Who would live and die a slave?

The Curious Nature of Elections

In democratic countries, the government holds elections to decide on difficult issues. The majority view generally rules. We don't make decisions through street fights or wars. Today when you think of elections, you probably think of equal voting rights, accurate voters' lists, a **secret ballot**, and a quiet, orderly process. But elections in British North America were nothing like that:

• Only males who owned property could vote. Women and Aboriginals could not vote.
• People lived far from each other, so they had to travel to vote. Elections took place over days and weeks.
• There were no secret ballots. In most cases people had to shout their choice, often in front of other people.
• Polling stations were placed near taverns or "hospitality suites" run by candidates. Bribing with food and drinks was common. Drunkenness often turned polling stations into battlegrounds.
• Voters' lists were often inaccurate and people residing in cemeteries were known to rise miraculously to vote.
• Bullying and intimidation were common and it was possible to force a vote since there was no secret ballot.

Today, most of these practices are against the law. Secret ballots were first used in Australia, and were introduced in Canada in 1874. They made elections freer, although bribery went on well into the 20th century in some parts of Canada.

• Rebellion in Lower Canada

The rebellions in Lower Canada made the radicals in Upper Canada even more eager to fight. They knew they weren't alone in their cause. How could the British defeat two rebellions in two colonies at once? When battles broke out in Lower Canada in November of 1837, Bond Head sent all his troops. Upper Canada was undefended and in December of that year, Mackenzie felt it was time to strike.

Many men were eager to defeat a government they felt did not represent them, but they weren't really ready for war. Take a look at this sketch. How can you tell that these men are not well prepared to fight a battle?

◄ Playback ►

1. Place in order from most serious to least serious the short-term causes of the rebellion in Upper Canada. Briefly explain your choice of most important cause.

2. Elections of the time were often a problem instead of a solution to a political issue. Explain why.

3. If you had lived in Upper Canada would you have taken up arms against the government? Why or why not?

4. Is violence ever acceptable when trying to win political change? Explain.

THE MARCH DOWN YONGE STREET

Ready to strike against the British, Mackenzie called his supporters together early in December. They were to meet at Montgomery's Tavern, then march down Yonge Street to seize the government. About 1,000 men gathered at the tavern. Many were poorly equipped and unprepared for a revolt, and nobody really knew what to do. Mackenzie was a great speaker, but not much of an organizer or a leader.

BATTLE OF TORONTO

In the meantime, retired army officer Colonel Moodie watched the men flood into Toronto to meet Mackenzie. He knew that the city and government were practically undefended, with troops already sent to Lower Canada. Moodie and others loyal to the British connection saddled their horses and headed down Yonge Street to find and warn Governor Bond Head. But their path was blocked by armed guards and a barricade. Moodie was determined to get through. Shots rang out, Moodie fired, but was hit and died.

A Toronto alderman, John Powell, was captured by the rebels. He killed his captor and escaped to warn the governor, and Bond Head got his forces ready. But Mackenzie was still disorganized. He delayed his attack. Some rebels left for home as others arrived. A group of rebels faced off against a group of loyalists but both groups ran from the battlefield in opposite directions. So far, the battle wasn't much to write about.

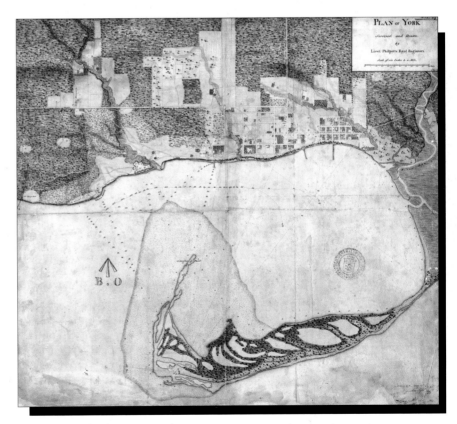

Map of York, 1837

Citizens rushed to defend Toronto from the rebels. They quickly defeated Mackenzie's forces. In your opinion, what was the rebels' greatest weakness?

Here's how Mackenzie described the chaos of the Battle of Toronto:

Colonel Lount and those in the front fired — and instead of stepping to one side to make room for those behind to fire, fell flat on their faces. The next rank did the same thing. Many of the country people, when they saw the riflemen in front falling down and heard the firing, they imagined that those who fell were killed by the enemy's fire, and took to their heels. This was almost too much for the human patience. The city would have been ours in an hour, probably without firing a shot. But 800 ran, and unfortunately the wrong way.

A VERY SHORT WAR

As people left or ran off in the wrong direction, the rebel forces were dwindling. More loyalist citizens were arriving, trying to defend their government until the army could get there. Mackenzie was acting stranger and stranger. At one point he even held a pistol to the head of his own military chief who had suggested an immediate withdrawal. Bond Head's forces

DEFEAT IN THE WEST

Rebellion in Upper Canada wasn't just confined to Toronto. Rebels were getting ready to battle over similar issues in the southwest of the colony, near present-day London, Ontario. Dr. Charles Duncombe organized several hundred rebels at Sodom, Ontario, and prepared to march on Brantford, Ontario. News of the rebel force reached Colonel Allan McNab. He soon gathered a loyalist force of about 2,000, including Six Nations warriors. They quickly scattered Duncombe's rebels and captured nearly 500 of them. The loyalist force crushed the rebellion for good by burning the rebels' farms.

Duncombe's western rebellion was short-lived and like Mackenzie, he fled to the United States.

marched to Montgomery's Tavern where they quickly dispersed the rebels by firing 1,000 muskets and two cannons.

Just as in Lower Canada, the rebellion's leaders weren't much help. Mackenzie fled to the United States hoping to get more military and financial support to overthrow the government. Samuel Lount and Peter Matthews, high-ranking supporters of Mackenzie, were soon captured. In fact, even the army wasn't much help. An army of citizen-soldiers had sprung up to defend the government from an army of rebels, turning the rebellion into a civil war between neighbours. The effect of the conflict would last for generations. The term "rebel" became a dirty word in the politics of the colony.

NAVY ISLAND

William Lyon Mackenzie refused to give up. He and a few followers seized Navy Island, a 130-square-kilometre island in the Niagara River, and proclaimed it to be the capital of an independent Republic of Upper Canada. They conducted a few minor raids on Upper Canada hoping to defeat government forces, but were soon arrested by American officials who wanted to avoid conflict with Britain.

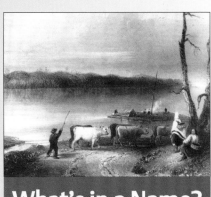

What's in a Name?

Navy Island got its name because its forests once provided timber for the ships of the Royal Navy. In 1945, it was proposed as the site for the headquarters of the newly created United Nations. Instead, New York City became the U.N. home.

Josiah Henson

UPPER CANADA'S BLACK DEFENDERS

One community that didn't want to see American-style changes to the colonies was the Black community. Many Black people had fought for the British during the American War of Independence and the War of 1812. During the time of the rebellions, many had escaped slavery in the U.S. and come to freedom in the colonies using the safe houses of the **Underground Railroad**. They were loyal to this government that had saved them, and they worried that the rebels would bring slavery to Canada or send former slaves back home.

Within a month of the outbreak of rebellion in the colonies, 1,000 Black people volunteered for service. Together, they formed a unit of Black troops called the Coloured Corps, led by former slave Josiah Henson. The Coloured Corps took part in the attack on rebel forces on Navy Island and the dramatic torching and sinking of the American steamer *Caroline*.

Black troops were among the forces that drove Mackenzie's rebels from Navy Island in the Niagara River. The sinking of the American steamer *Caroline*, a rebel supply vessel, ended the occupation of the island.

Its members were reliable defenders of the colony during the rebellions and for years after. While others deserted from army life, Black Canadians remained loyal to this new land.

End of a Rebel Dream

Mackenzie believed in his dream, but others could see that any reform to Upper Canada's politics wasn't going to come from the barrel of a gun. Mackenzie's poorly organized rebellion was quickly crushed. Very few people wanted to follow him on the road to war. Most of the rebels faded back into their remote settlements. The major leaders escaped to the U.S. or were captured. Although American sympathizers would keep raiding and invading Upper Canada for a few years, the rebellion was dead. The next chapter in the politics of Upper Canada would be written in ink, not blood.

The rebel flag featured two white stars on a deep blue background. The stars were to represent the independent states of Upper and Lower Canada. However, the Union Jack was destined to fly over the colonies for some time yet.

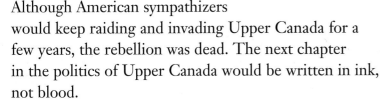

1. **In your view which was the most important battle of the rebellion in Upper Canada? Why?**

2. **What appear to be the strengths and weaknesses of the rebels and loyalists?**

3. **How would you account for the defeat of the rebels?**

4. **In your view how should the rebels have been treated when the fighting was finished? Explain.**

History in Action — Political Posters

The Back Story

Elections in British North America in the 1830s were heated, and often became violent. Politicians were always ready to attack their rivals aloud or in print. In 1836, in Toronto, the Tories, led by Governor Bond Head, and the radical reformers, led by William Lyon Mackenzie, were vying for people's votes.

The Goal

Imagine that you are going to a political meeting in Toronto during the election of 1836. With a partner, design and create an attractive, attention-getting poster that you can bring with you to the meeting.

The Steps

1. Review the material that you have studied to make sure that you understand the major issues and personalities in the politics of Upper Canada. Ask questions about anything that you do not understand.
2. Decide whether you want to play the role of a Tory, a reformer, or a radical.
3. Complete a rough draft of your poster, considering size, colour, image, slogan, and design.
4. Show your draft to peers and family for ideas and suggestions.
5. Make any necessary revisions and create your final poster.
6. On the back of your poster, write a few paragraphs explaining your poster and why you think it is effective.
7. Place your poster on a bulletin board. Be prepared to discuss it with your peers.

Evaluating Your Work

These are the criteria you should think about as you complete your work. Your work should:

- Be neatly and carefully designed
- Be original
- Be historically accurate
- Include a brief written commentary on the back

CHAPTER 4

BATTLE LOST, WAR WON

The rebellions were over. Hundreds had been killed by British troops in Lower Canada. Unprepared rebels in Upper Canada were defeated by loyalist citizens before the army could even get there. The rebel leaders were dead, in jail, banished, or in exile. It was obvious that war wouldn't bring political change. Change did come eventually, and within 10 years, nearly all of the goals of the rebels had been achieved.

Public executions of rebels took place in both colonies. While some people were ready for revenge, many soon forgot and even forgave the rebels for their actions.

Telling Their Stories

Watch *Canada: A People's History*, Episode 7: "Rebellion and Reform, The Calm Between the Storms" (hr. 2, 16:25 to 26:44). Even though the rebellion had been broken, some men continued to fight. Watch their story and write a paragraph explaining what you think it meant to be a rebel, and why you think they would continue to think that rebellion was the only way to bring change.

This rebel raid near Windsor, late in 1838, was beaten back by forces loyal to Britain and the government of Upper Canada. Americans who surrendered were shot on capture.

"Four rebels captured; shot accordingly."
Colonel John Prince

PUNISHMENT

The government wasn't just going to let the rebellions die. Attacking the government was a serious crime. To show its power and teach the rebels a lesson, the government executed many rebels. Others were sent to jail or into exile. In 1838, though, **pardons** were granted to minor participants and by the 1840s, all rebels were allowed to return to Canada under a general **amnesty**.

One rebel, the Chevalier de Lorimier, died with these words:

> *I have only a few hours left to live but I wish to share this precious time between my religious duties and those I owe my compatriots; for them I die the inglorious death of the common murderer; for them I leave behind my young children and my wife who have no means of support, and for them I die crying: Long live freedom! Long live independence!*

REBELLION LIVES ON

With the rebellions over, it should have been time for peace and calm in the colonies. But there were still security threats, this time from secret organizations called Hunters' Lodges. When Mackenzie fled to the United States he and other rebels found lots of support for their cause. Many Americans were angry about British control of Canada and

In 1840, terrorists blew up Brock's Monument in Queenston, Upper Canada. Brock was a British hero of the War of 1812. The 41-metre-high structure was shattered. The bombers were never caught. The monument was rebuilt and still looks over the Niagara frontier today.

hadn't forgotten their own War of Independence, or the War of 1812.

About 5,000 men joined these Hunters' Lodges, which were set up somewhat like terrorist cells today. These men unleashed small, savage raids along the U.S. border with the colonies for several years. They and other American groups seized and burned Canadian and British ships on the Great Lakes. With each raid, there was swift, brutal reaction from loyalist Canadian forces. Raiders were executed or deported to Van Diemen's Land in Tasmania. Eventually American officials, who didn't want another war with Britain, were able to break up the Hunters' Lodges.

◀ Playback ▶

1. **What evidence is there that rebellion did not end with the defeats of 1837–1838?**

2. **What were the Hunters' Lodges and what was their purpose?**

3. **Explain why you think terrorists target public buildings.**

NEXT STEPS

When the shooting died down, British North America still had to find a way to solve its political problems. The people had rejected rebellion, but they knew things had to change. In most of the colonies, the calls for reform slowly increased. Soon the moderate reformers brought their ideas forward. They knew the British government would rather talk to them than fight again.

UNITING THE CANADAS

The British appointed John George Lambton, Lord Durham, as Governor General, and sent him to the colonies to find solutions to the rebellions. His 1839 report included three major recommendations:

1. Unite the two rebellious colonies of Upper and Lower Canada.
2. Allow responsible government for the colonies in their local affairs.
3. Pursue a union of all the British North American colonies.

Lord Durham

In Durham's opinion, the French were inferior and the colonies should be English. If the two Canadas were united, the French would become weaker in Parliament and Canada's economy would become stronger.

Naturally, French Canada was not pleased with Durham's opinion, or with his attempt to take away its identity. The Family Compact and Château Clique were upset with the possibility of responsible government. The British liked the first recommendation, though. In 1841, the two colonies were united in the Act of Union: one colony, one governor, one assembly, and one language, English.

A FRENCH-ENGLISH ALLIANCE

In the United Province of Canada, government reform would come through the work of Robert Baldwin and Louis-Hippolyte LaFontaine.

Baldwin was from a wealthy Toronto family that believed in reform. Baldwin was elected to the Assembly and then appointed to the Executive Council, but he disagreed so strongly with the

Robert Baldwin

Louis-Hippolyte LaFontaine

Council's lack of responsibility to the Assembly that he resigned. In Baldwin's opinion, the only way to get responsibility was to have a reformist majority in the House of Assembly. To do that, he would need to form an alliance with French Canada. He sent a letter to LaFontaine, a French member of the Assembly.

LaFontaine was already fighting for the changes he knew were needed in Lower Canada. When Britain agreed to the Act of Union, LaFontaine had an even bigger fight — saving the French-Canadian way of life. Although he was a member of the Parti Patriote, he did not believe in forcing change through rebellion. Baldwin's idea of an alliance seemed to him like the right solution.

CHANGE IN NOVA SCOTIA

In Nova Scotia, the push for change came from Joseph Howe, the publisher of the *Novascotian*. In 1836, he was elected to the legislature and proposed a list of resolutions for political change.

TESTING THE ALLIANCE

The Baldwin-LaFontaine alliance was proof that real change for the people of Canada would come from the French and English working together. But the alliance almost died before it got started. In the new colony's first elections, LaFontaine ran in the riding he had always represented. But the polling station was near an English town, and he and his supporters were kept from voting. LaFontaine lost his seat. Without him, the majority alliance would fail, and the reformers wouldn't be able to push for change.

Robert Baldwin's father was also a politician. Baldwin asked his father to resign and to let LaFontaine run in his place. His father agreed, and LaFontaine was elected in the English riding of North York. A year later, Robert Baldwin was elected in the French riding of Rimouski.

Bicultural Partnership

Relations between the English and the French in the united province had often been strained, but Baldwin and LaFontaine were friends and allies, and they presented a model for political unity. Their message and example of **bicultural** partnership is part of an important Canadian tradition.

Louis-Hippolyte LaFontaine:

"It is in the interest of the reformers of both provinces to come together in the legislature, in a spirit of peace, union, friendship and fraternity. United action is needed now more than ever."

Robert Baldwin:

"There is, and must be no question of races. It were madness on one side, and guilt, deep guilt on both to make such a question. The Reformers of Upper Canada are ready to make every allowance for the unfortunate state of things and are resolved, as I believe them to be, to unite with their Lower Canadian Brethren cordially as friends, and to afford every assistance in obtaining justice."

THE FINAL STEPS TO RESPONSIBLE GOVERNMENT

In the mid-1800s, Britain entered into **free-trade** agreements with many countries and didn't need to dominate the economy of the colonies any more. Britain granted the colonies the power of self-government. The people of the colonies elected Reformers to represent them.

In 1847, Joseph Howe's party won the election in Nova Scotia and became the first responsible government in the colonies.

That same year, Lord Elgin, the son-in-law of Lord Durham, became Governor General. He was wealthy and privileged, but rather than support the Family Compact and Château Clique, he worked with the Reformers toward their goal of responsible government. In 1848, the Reformers won the elections in the United Province of Canada. Lord Elgin asked Baldwin and LaFontaine to form a government. The two leaders successfully fought to end restrictions on the use of French in Parliament, and continued their struggle for change.

Joseph Howe

Lord Elgin

Responsible Governments

1847 Nova Scotia
1848 The United Province of Canada
1851 Prince Edward Island
1854 New Brunswick
1855 Newfoundland

One Last Eruption

The first bill the new Reform government put forward was controversial: the Rebellion Losses Bill. It would reimburse people who suffered losses during the recent rebellions.

The people of the province had elected the Reformers and the Reformers put forward the bill. If Lord Elgin really believed in responsible government, he would have to agree to the bill and sign it into law. Tory supporters were outraged. Why would their government help those people who were active in rebelling against it?

In 1849, Tory supporters burnt down the Parliament Buildings to stop Lord Elgin from signing the Rebellion Losses Bill. Soon after, the government decided Montreal was too dangerous a place for the Parliament Buildings, and moved the capital to Toronto.

Once again, violence erupted in Montreal, the capital of the Province of Canada. Tory supporters headed into the streets. They attacked Elgin's carriage and destroyed the houses of many Reformers, including LaFontaine. In a night of rioting, protesters set the Parliament Buildings of Canada on fire and destroyed them.

Lord Elgin signed the bill in 1849, and made responsible government a reality in the United Province of Canada.

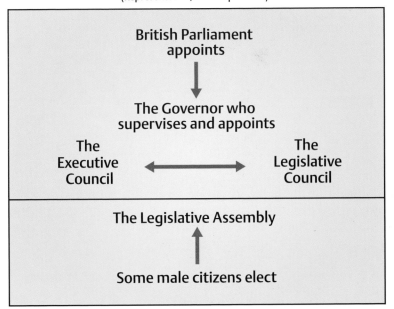

Colonial Government in British North America
(Representative, Not Responsible)

British Parliament
appoints

The Governor who
supervises and appoints

The
Executive
Council ⟷ The
Legislative
Council

The Legislative Assembly

Some male citizens elect

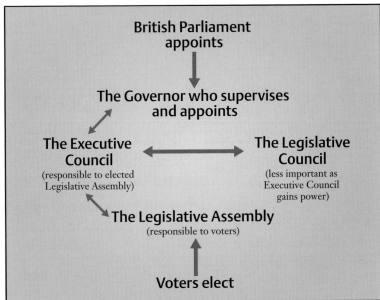

Responsible Government
(Governor Responsible to Elected Representatives)

British Parliament
appoints

The Governor who supervises
and appoints

The Executive
Council
(responsible to elected
Legislative Assembly) ⟷ The Legislative
Council
(less important as
Executive Council
gains power)

The Legislative Assembly
(responsible to voters)

Voters elect

A diagram showing the old government of the colonies, which was representative government. Below that is a diagram of the new government, which was responsible government. In this new model, the executive is responsible to the representatives that the people elect, not to the British government.

REBELLION, REFORM, AND THE FIRST NATIONS

What had been happening to the Aboriginal people during this time? Many had been weakened by disease, war, and the flood of new settlers into their territories. Few adapted well to the restrictions of life on reserves. Most political leaders, concerned with changes in their own society, didn't think about the needs or wants of Aboriginals. Yet some Aboriginals were strong supporters of loyalist forces, and they helped defend the colony of Upper Canada from border raids. Lord Durham, as this painting shows, did meet with Aboriginal leaders to seek their opinion on changes in Upper Canada.

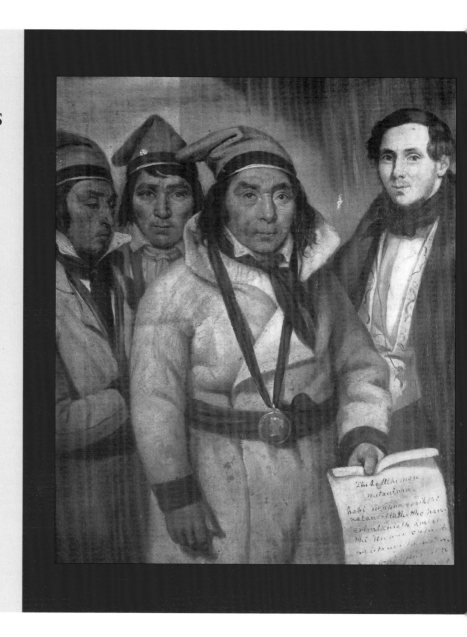

THE ANNEXATION MOVEMENT

Some people were so opposed to responsible government and Britain's new policy of free trade that they wanted to cut ties to Britain completely. Instead, they saw the United States as their new partner.

In 1849, a small but powerful group of people began to promote the idea of **annexation**, or union with the Americans. These people thought Canada's economy would collapse without automatic access to British markets, and they were angry over payouts from the Rebellion Losses Bill. In their opinion, Canada's future lay to the south, and not to a Britain that seemed to reject their loyalty. They held meetings, published pamphlets, and called for "a friendly and peaceful separation from the British connection and a union upon equitable terms with the North America Confederacy." These new "loyalists" wanted to abandon Canada and join the United States. However, the Canadiens of Canada East and the farming communities of Canada West were not interested. The annexation movement soon collapsed.

Loosening the Ties

With responsible government, the ties of British North America to Britain were loosened, but not cut. The colonies now had full control of local affairs, but ties with the rest of the world were still in British hands. Most people were happy to be part of this British Empire, and it would be many years before the call would come for full political independence.

◄ Playback ►

1. **Briefly describe the role Baldwin, LaFontaine, and Howe played in the winning of responsible government.**

2. **What role did Lord Durham and Lord Elgin play in the winning of responsible government?**

3. **In your view, should Lord Elgin have signed the Rebellion Losses Bill? Explain.**

4. **What is your personal reaction to the annexation movement? Do you think Canada will ever join the United States? Explain.**

5. **In your view what was the most important event on the road to responsible government? Explain fully.**

History in Action — Memo to Lord Elgin

The Back Story

In 1848, Robert Baldwin and Louis-Hippolyte LaFontaine proposed the Rebellion Losses Bill to reimburse those who had lost property during the rebellions in Lower Canada.

Many Tories were violently opposed, and felt that their government had no right to support the bill. But Reformers were in favour, and they were the people who had elected the government. The decision to sign the bill was a very difficult one for Lord Elgin, the Governor General of the colony.

The Goal

Imagine that you are a member of the Legislative Assembly of the United Province of Canada. Decide whether you are in favour of or opposed to the Rebellion Losses Bill. Write a one-page memo to Lord Elgin supporting your opinion and indicating what you think the results of passing the bill will be. Urge Lord Elgin to take your advice.

The decision to sign the Rebellion Losses Bill into law was a clear victory for responsible government but it resulted in an explosion of violence.

The Steps

1. Reread this chapter to review what you know about responsible government. Ask your teacher or a classmate to explain anything you do not understand.
2. Decide whether you are going to be a Reformer or a Tory.
3. Make a point-form plan noting the major strengths and weaknesses of passing the Rebellion Losses Bill.
4. Draft a memo to Lord Elgin, stating your decision and supporting your argument.
5. Review and revise your first draft.
6. Be prepared to share the final version of your memo orally with other members of the Assembly (your class).

Evaluating Your Work

Think about these criteria as you complete your work.
Your work should:
- Clearly indicate your recommendation
- Offer several arguments to support your recommendation
- Be at least one page in length and neatly written or word-processed
- Include both a rough draft and a final version
- Be presented in a clear and confident manner

CHAPTER 5

FAST FORWARD

The fog of war has long drifted away since the rebellions in 1837. Rebellion was but one step on the long journey to nationhood. Most Canadians have trouble remembering the names of Papineau, Mackenzie, Durham, and Elgin. However the impact of the drive for political reform has marked and changed Canada forever. Some of the issues raised so long ago continue to trouble Canada and the world.

FIGHTING FOR CHANGE

Change continues in Canada today. Many First Nations groups are trying to protect their claims on land or their traditions of hunting, logging, and fishing in the places where they live. First Nations continue to negotiate these

In September 1999, the Supreme Court of Canada granted traditional fishing rights to 34 First Nations groups. In New Brunswick, that meant that Native fishers had the right to catch lobster out of season. Other fishers were not happy.

In October, 150 fishing boats headed into Miramichi Bay to protest the decision. But the protest turned violent, and Native traps, equipment, and fish plants were vandalized.

As far away as British Columbia, other First Nations showed their support by blockading a CP Rail line. How does blockading roads or rail lines help force change? Why do you think First Nations bands in B.C. would support those on the East Coast? How could change for one band affect other bands?

rights with the federal government, but negotiations take time, and sometimes emotions take over. Road blockades and angry gatherings have happened from coast to coast as people try to resolve the issues.

THE EMERGENCE OF TERRORISM

Today, we would call some of the events of the rebellions "acts of terrorism." These include shootings, burning of property, bombings, and so on. In 1837–1838, Canada rejected terrorism as a way to bring political change. However, terrorism is the way that many try to bring political change in other countries today, and Canada chooses to help fight terrorism. Canadians were horrified by the terrorist attacks on the World Trade Center Towers in New York on September 11, 2001. Canadian forces played a direct role in the war on terrorism when they were sent to Afghanistan in 2002. Canada has pledged its support in the ongoing war against terrorism to the United Nations and our allies such as Great Britain and the United States.

CANADIENS TO QUÉBÉCOIS

The rebellion in Upper Canada was focused mainly on government. In Lower Canada, though, the key issue for many people was the survival of French language, religion, and culture. Many Patriotes worried about the survival of their very identity. While others in British North America saw themselves as British, most in Lower Canada saw themselves as Canadiens. They were the descendants of Champlain and Cartier. They didn't look to France for their identity. They looked inward to themselves and the society they had built on the banks of the St. Lawrence. They remembered the glories of New France and struggled to keep their Catholic faith, French language, and Canadien identity. Many Patriotes were quite prepared to fight for total independence. Some were even prepared to join the United States rather than live under British rule, laws, and customs.

A separatist supporter holds the Quebec flag during the referendum of 1995.

The desire to preserve a unique identity has never faltered among French Canadians. Today, many francophones in the province of Quebec reject the term "Canadiens" and refer to themselves as Québécois, looking to Quebec as the birthplace of their community. While many Québécois are quite happy to be seen as Canadians too, others embrace the dreams of independence and have a fear of being swept away in an English sea. Separatism has been a central issue for Canadians and their leaders for nearly 50 years. Two political parties based in Quebec, the Bloc Québécois and the Parti Québécois, are peaceful heirs to the Patriotes of Papineau. Quebeckers have faced two votes about leaving Confederation, on May 20, 1980 and on Oct. 30, 1995. In 1995, the people voted to stay by a margin of less than one percent. The future of Canada–Quebec relations is likely to be difficult and some of the issues and fears of 1837–1838 are not yet laid to rest.

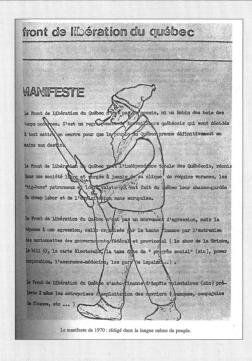

Le manifeste de 1970 : rédigé dans la langue même du peuple.

While the vast majority of Québécois abhor violence, a small number have been prepared to use terror to win the dream of independence. In the late 1960s and early 1970s, a small terrorist organization, the Front de Libération du Québec (FLQ), unleashed a campaign of violence in Quebec. Members robbed banks, planted bombs, organized kidnappings, and murdered one member of the Quebec cabinet. They were crushed and rejected by nearly all Canadians, both English and French. The fact that they looked to history for inspiration is shown in the use of the famous drawing of an old Canadien fighting in 1837, which they placed on their FLQ letterhead. One of these terrorist "cells" was called "Chenier" after the doctor who died in the fiery battle at St. Eustache.

CLOSER TIES WITH THE U.S.

Only a few of the rebels in 1837–1838 favoured union with the United States. Most people in all the colonies treasured the British connection and were often fiercely anti-American. Historically, however, Canada's British connection has grown weaker while our connection to our powerful neighbour to the south has grown far stronger. We have been allies in many world conflicts. We are active trading partners with each other. We share many of the same popular public figures. We travel widely and freely in one another's countries. For some beyond North America, we may seem almost identical. Whether or not we become one nation in the future, it is clear that we are likely to share many more and deeper connections.

EVOLUTION NOT REVOLUTION

Canadian history shows that, in general, Canadians have chosen the path of evolution — slow, measured change — rather than revolution, which suggests dramatic, wholesale, even violent change. Some say that Canadian history is

Responsible Government Lost

Now that you know about the struggle for responsible government, you might find it hard to believe that one colony actually gave up that right after having it for years. The Great Depression (which began in 1929) and local corruption nearly caused the complete collapse of Newfoundland's economy. Newfoundland, which was still a British colony, chose to end responsible government and accept more direction and help from Great Britain. The British installed a Commission of Government and appointed representatives from England to oversee the colony's affairs. The economy was stabilized, and after the outbreak of World War II, Newfoundland participated actively and importantly in the Allied war effort. When the war was over, Newfoundlanders wanted another direction. In a series of **referenda**, they had to choose between union with the United States, continuing the Commission of Government, or union with Canada. In 1949, after a bitter and extremely close **referendum** vote, Newfoundland entered Confederation as Canada's tenth province. In 2001, the province changed its name officially to Newfoundland and Labrador.

Newfoundland joins Confederation in 1949 with this signature from Joey Smallwood.

boring because much of our past is built on compromises and complex political documents, rather than glorious battles and military heroes. On the other hand, revolutions often result in destruction and casualties. Reason is usually replaced by passion. As well, countries that choose revolution may be tempted to return to drama and violence to solve other problems, while a society developed more slowly and peacefully might be expected to reject violence and prefer to change peacefully. One prime minister noted that revolution leaves a heritage of iron while evolution leaves a heritage of gold.

Governor General Adrienne Clarkson gives an Order of Canada.

The Governor General: A Changing Office

The role of governor general has been important in Canada's history. The first governor general was French explorer Samuel de Champlain. Lord Durham and Lord Elgin were the governors general who helped bring responsible government to the colonies. The office of governor general has changed radically but it is still central in the political and social life of Canada today. Once appointed in France and later England, governors general today are usually Canadians appointed by the British monarch on the advice of the Canadian prime minister. Duties of Canada's current governor general include the following:

- Representing the British Crown in Canada
- Providing "royal assent" to bills passed by the House of Commons and Senate so that the bills can become law
- Serving as a ceremonial Head of State for Canada
- Awarding medals and decorations, such as the Order of Canada, to Canadians
- Reading the Speech from the Throne at the official opening of a session of Parliament

Canadian Government Today

Today you live under a system of government that you can trace back hundreds of years. A series of reforms and changes have gradually shaped the political life of your Canada. You have inherited the changes of the past and maybe you will play a role in shaping the changes of the future.

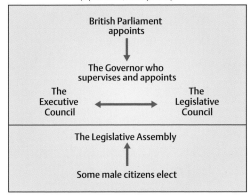

Colonial Government in British North America
(Representative, Not Responsible)

British Parliament appoints

The Governor who supervises and appoints

The Executive Council ⟷ The Legislative Council

The Legislative Assembly

Some male citizens elect

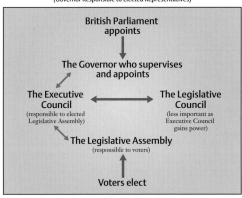

Responsible Government
(Governor Responsible to Elected Representatives)

British Parliament appoints

The Governor who supervises and appoints

The Executive Council (responsible to elected Legislative Assembly) ⟷ The Legislative Council (less important as Executive Council gains power)

The Legislative Assembly (responsible to voters)

Voters elect

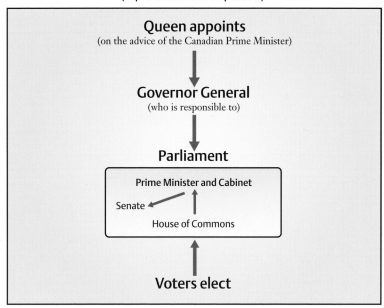

Government in Canada Today
(Representative and Responsible)

Queen appoints
(on the advice of the Canadian Prime Minister)

Governor General
(who is responsible to)

Parliament

Prime Minister and Cabinet

Senate ← House of Commons

Voters elect

This series of diagrams demonstrates Canada's slow approach to political change. Evolution not revolution has marked most of Canadian history. What future changes to Canada's government can you imagine?

◀ Playback ▶

1. Do you think Quebec will continue to be a part of Canada in the future? Explain.

2. What evidence is there that the United States and Canada have become closer friends since the Rebellions of 1837–1838? In your view, how likely is it that Canada and the United States will remain separate nations? Explain fully.

3. What is the difference between evolution and revolution? Which approach has marked most of Canadian history?

4. If you could change any part of Canada's system of government what would it be and why?

5. What role do you see yourself playing as an adult citizen in Canada?

History in Action
Analyzing Causes and Results

The Back Story

When we study the past, we need to be able to identify clearly the important causes and results of events. A cause is something that moves or influences something to happen. A result is something that follows or is the outcome of an action or event.

The Goal

You will write several paragraphs to explain what you think were the three most important causes and the three most important events of the Rebellions of 1837–1838, supporting your opinion with details from this book.

The Steps

1. Review the list below. Then create a two-column chart with the headings "Cause" and "Result." Sort the information into the correct column.
   - William Lyon Mackenzie
   - Lord Durham
   - Canals versus Roads
   - Family Compact and Château Clique
   - British Immigration to Lower Canada
   - Hunters' Lodges
   - Responsible Government
   - Patriotes
   - Exile
   - Rebellion Losses Bill
2. Review in this book the material about the information you have sorted.
3. Decide what you think were the three most important causes and the three most important results of the Rebellions of 1837–1838.
4. Write two separate paragraphs to explain your choices, supporting your work with details. Be prepared to share your findings with your classmates.

Identifying causes and results of historical events can be difficult. Names, dates, documents, and complex events can be confusing.

Evaluating Your Work

Think about these criteria as you complete your work. Your work should:
- Include your chart and your completed paragraphs
- Clearly identify three important causes and three important results of the Rebellions of 1837–1838
- Include details that support your opinion
- Be checked for grammar, spelling, and punctuation
- Be presented clearly and persuasively

Glossary

amnesty a decision by a government to pardon or grant freedom to a large group of individual, such as political prisoners

anglophone a person who speaks English, especially in a country where two or more languages are spoken

annexation to take possession of a country or an area of land, usually without permission or by force

bee a gathering of people for a specific purpose

bicultural relating to or including two distinct cultures

boycott to refuse to deal with a person or organization, to buy a product or take part in an activity, in order to express disapproval or to force acceptance of certain conditions

British North America all British possessions in and adjacent to North and South America

Canadien a French Canadian

cholera a bacterial infection of the bowels, causing severe diarrhea and sometimes death

clique a small, exclusive group of people with common interests, views, or purposes who do not want other people to join the group

duel a formal fight using weapons, usually guns or swords, fought between two people in the presence of witnesses

exile a period of forced or voluntary absence from one's country or home, especially for political reasons

expulsion being forced to leave a place or organization by official action, usually with the loss of rights or privileges

francophone someone who speaks French as the first or sometimes second language

free trade buying and selling of goods between countries without limits on the amount and without special taxes on the goods

governor general the main representative of the British king or queen in another country which is controlled by Britain

libel a piece of writing that states false or harmful things about a person, or the legal claim made in court that accuses someone of writing such things

Loyalist in British North America, someone who is or remains loyal to the British Crown

loyalist someone who strongly supports the government or ruler in power

pardon to officially forgive someone who has committed a crime and to release them from punishment

politics the activities of the government, organizations, and people who try to influence the way a country is governed

polling station the place where people vote in a political election

recession a period of reduced business activity when the economy of a country is not doing well and there is a lot of un-employment

referendum (pl. **referenda**) a vote in which all the people in a country or an area give their opinion about or decide on an important political or social issue

Glossary

representative government government in which the number of elected members in the legislature is based on the population of an area

sack to steal all the valuable things from a place and destroy it, usually during a war

secret ballot a printed ballot on which the names of all the candidates appear, the ballot is marked by the voter in secret

sedition the attempt to persuade other people to oppose the government, sometimes by using violence

seigneur a member of the nobility who owns a large estate in New France granted to him by the king of France; a feudal lord

seigneury the land and manor house in New France granted to the nobility, the church, or the military by the king of France

tenant farmer a farmer who works land owned by another and pays rent for the use of the land

Underground Railroad a system of safe homes and routes, created by people who were against slavery, to help slaves escape from the southern United States to the North or to Canada in the 1860s.

Index

Credits

Page 1: Government of Ontario Art Collection; Page 2 top: National Archives of Canada, C-40162, bottom: National Archives of Canada, C-073725; Page 3 top: *The Habitant Farm* by Cornelius Krieghoff, National Gallery of Canada, 2036, bottom: Courtesy of Steve Taylor and Views of the Famine, http://vassun.vassar.edu/sttaylor/FAMINE/; Page 4 top: National Archives of Canada, c-044633, left/bottom: Grand Trunk Railway Locomotive No. 162, National Gallery of Canada, 21303; Page 5, clockwise from top: National Archives of Canada, C-016551, National Archives of Canada, C-12649, National Archives of Canada, C-000578, National Archives of Canada, c-002366, *A View of the Château-Richer, Cape Torment*, and *Lower end of the Isle of Orleans near Quebec*, by Thomas Davies, National Gallery of Canada, 6275; Page 6: National Archives of Canada, C-40162; Page 7: Darrell McCalla; Page 10: National Archives of Canada, C-013449; Page 11: *Cholera Plague, Quebec*, by Joseph Légaré, National Gallery of Canada, 7157; Page 12: National Archives of Canada, C-073707; Page 14 left to right: National Archives of Canada, C-003305, National Archives of Canada, C-005968, National Archives of Canada, C-007044; Page 15: CBC, *Canada: A People's History*; Page 16 left to right: National Archives of Canada, C-024937, National Archives of Canada, C-005435, National Archives of Canada, C-054305; Page 17 top: MTL T16969, bottom: Archives nationales du Québec, P600-61GH-272-63; Page 18 left to right: © Public Domain *Roughing it in the Bush, or Life in Canada* by Susanna Moodie, 1st ed. London: R. Bentley, 1852., National Library of Canada, NL-15557; Page 19 left to right: © Public Domain *The Backwoods of Canada* by Catherine Parr Traill. 1st ed. London: C. Knight 1836, National Archives of Canada, C-067337; Page 20: Archives of Ontario, 10008043; Page 21 National Archives of Ontario, C-013392; Page 22 Bibliothéque nationale du Québec; Page 23 National Archives of Canada, C-117310; Page 24 left to right: CBC, *Canada: A People's History*, National Archives of Canada, C-003653; Page 25: National Archives of Canada, C-018294; Page 26: National Archives of Canada, C-000393; Page 27 left to right: National Archives of Canada, C-000396, National Archives of Canada, C-018456, National Archives of Canada, C-133484; Page 28: National Archives of Canada, C-073725; Page 29: National Archives of Canada, C-004783; Page 30 top: National Archives of Canada, C-041467, bottom: Canadian Heritage Gallery; Page 31: William Morris fonds, Queen's University Archives Locator 2139, Box 2; Page 32: Charles William Jefferys, *Rebels of 1837 Drilling in North York, 1898*, Art Gallery of Ontario; Page 33: National Archives of Canada, NMC-17026; Page 34: National Archives of Canada, C-004782; Page 35 top: National Archives of Canada, C-004500, bottom: National Archives of Canada, C-040724; Page 36 top: Documenting the American South (http://docsouth.unc.edu), The University of North Carolina at Chapel Hill Libraries, bottom: National Archives of Canada, C-004788, Page 39: National Archives of Canada, C-013493: Page 40 top: CBC, *Canada: A People's History*; bottom: Parks Canada Agency, Fort Malden National Historic Site of Canada; Page 41 left to right: National Archives of Canada, C-O11799, Geographical Visual Aids, Page 41 National Archives of Canada, C-121846; Page 43 left to right: National Archives of Canada, C-005962, National Archives of Canada, C-036094; Page 45 top: National Archives of Canada, C-054305, bottom: National Archives of Canada, C-018524; Page 46: National Archives of Canada, C-002726; Page 48: *Three Indian Chiefs and an Indian Agent* by Théophile Hamel, National Gallery of Canada; Page 50: National Archives of Canada, C-002726; Page 51: Keith Anderson ICP Photo Archive; Page 52: Ryan Remiorz / CP Photo Archive; Page 53 left to right: National Archives of Canada, C-017937, Bibliothéque nationale du Québec; Page 54: Ken Gigliotti / CP Photo Archive; Page 55: CP Photo Archive; Page 56: Jonathan Hayward / CP Photo Archive; Page 58: National Archive of Canada, C-002366.

Reviewers

Kathryn Brownell,
Terry Fox School,
Toronto, Ontario

Manny Calisto,
West St. Paul School,
West St. Paul, Manitoba

Greer Coe,
Montague Intermediate School,
Montague, Prince Edward Island

Rick Elliott,
John Buchan School,
Toronto, Ontario

Sheri Epstein,
Langstaff High School,
Thornhill, Ontario

Christine Greene,
Avalon East School Board,
St. John's, Newfoundland and Labrador

Joanne Wheeler,
St. Margaret School,
Calgary, Alberta

EXPLORERS AND PATHFINDERS

CANADA

A PEOPLE'S HISTORY

FIRST CONTACT

CANADA

A PEOPLE'S HISTORY

Also available in the series:

FIRST CONTACT

CANADA
A PEOPLE'S HISTORY

Aboriginal peoples had lived throughout North America for thousands of years. They had practiced a world view in which everyone shared the land and its resources. They viewed nature's resources as gifts, and they used these gifts wisely to ensure these resources would still be there for their children and their children's children to use.

Then, around 1600, Europeans began arriving in North America, bringing with them a world view that was very different from that of the Aboriginal peoples. To the newcomers, land was not something people shared. It was something people owned. The Europeans were interested in what they could gain from the land, the resources of that land, and the riches of the surrounding oceans.

In *First Contact*, we learn how over time, first fish, then furs, would bring the Europeans here to stay, and how those early encounters set the stage for a collision course between two very different sets of values—a clash that would change the lives of Aboriginal peoples forever.

Richly illustrated with maps, historical graphics, documents, paintings and portraits, *First Contact* examines the Aboriginal lifestyle before these first encounters, with special attention given to the traditions, customs, values, governments and spiritual beliefs.

The book explores the quest for riches that brought the early explorers—Christopher Columbus, John Cabot, Jacques Cartier and Samuel de Champlain—to Canada, the settlers who followed in search of a new life in the new land, and the arrival of missionaries intent on spreading Christianity around the world.

First Contact also explores the conflicts between the European nations as the quest for furs produced bitter rivalries and alliances.

The book concludes with an examination of Aboriginal peoples in Canada today, the on-going disputes over land claims, and debates over self-government.

Like other titles in this series, *First Contact* is based on and carefully linked to the popular CBC/Radio-Canada series, *Canada: A People's History*, available to schools across the country on video and DVD.

Dr. Cornelius J. Jaenen, Ph.D., LL.D., FRSC, is Professor Emeritus of History at the University of Ottawa. His numerous publications include *The Role of the Church in New France* (1976), *Friend and Foe* (1976), *Emerging Identities* (1986), *Les Franco-Ontariens* (1993), *The French Regime in the Upper Country* (1996), and *The Apostles' Doctrine and Fellowship: A Documentary History* (2003).

Fitzhenry & Whiteside

1-55041-443-7